IN
SPRING-
TIME

WESLEYAN POETRY

ALSO BY SARAH BLAKE

POETRY
Mr. West
Let's Not Live on Earth
Named After Death (chapbook)

NOVELS
Naamah
Clean Air

IN
SPRINGTIME

SARAH BLAKE

Wesleyan University Press   Middletown, Connecticut

Wesleyan University Press

Middletown CT 06459

www.wesleyan.edu/wespress

© 2023 Sarah Blake

Manufactured in the United States of America

Designed and composed in Adobe Caslon Pro by Sheryl P. Kober

Library of Congress Cataloging-in-Publication Data

Names: Blake, Sarah (poet), author.

Title: In springtime / Sarah Blake.

Description: Middletown, CT : Wesleyan University Press, [2023] | Series: Wesleyan poetry | Summary: "An epic poem of a survival examines what makes us human when removed from the human world, what identity means where it is a useless thing, and how loss shapes us"— Provided by publisher.

Identifiers: LCCN 2022031560 (print) | LCCN 2022031561 (ebook) | ISBN 9780819500250 (cloth) | ISBN 9780819500304 (trade paperback) | ISBN 9780819500311 (ebook)

Subjects: LCGFT: Poetry.

Classification: LCC PS3602.L3485 I5 2023 (print) | LCC PS3602.L3485 (ebook) | DDC 811/.6--dc23/eng/20220702

LC record available at https://lccn.loc.gov/2022031560

LC ebook record available at https://lccn.loc.gov/2022031561

5   4   3   2   1

FOR MY DAD

Contents

DAY 1

1.

Introductions: Horse. Dead bird. Mouse.

Though the horse won't stick around, will she?

The mouse—you won't know she's there unless you move the folded-up tarp that she's under with the garter snake.

Picture the dead bird how you will. She has a hole in her that an egg can squeeze out of (as if it's the egg's doing and not her big push).

Maybe the mouse will say something to you after all. She pities the bird. She wishes birds died and decayed in treetops.

Hiss, hiss, says the snake so softly no one can hear.

The mouse doesn't know much about decay. Surprisingly. The near rotten food in her belly.

God, there goes the horse, just like you thought.

2.

The horse's heart is not only larger than yours, but more round.
Like the moon. Like a peony. Like a child's head even.

Young doctors watch mouse heart transplants to learn the surgery
with hearts one thousand times larger.

You've walked around a dead mouse in your basement and you could
walk around a dead anything—giraffe, elephant, sperm whale on the
beach. There you are, an hour later, still on your feet.

But for now you're following the horse with her ridiculous globe
of a heart.

She leads you to water. Predictable. Horse-like.

It would be easy to forget about the dead bird except for how that
might have been you in the grass.

3.

How often you have thought that you were dying. Nearly every stomach virus or food poisoning. Looking back, it always passed quickly. And dying is probably not like vomiting, or the moments before vomiting when you try to hold that much sickness in your stomach.

Dying, up to this point, has shown itself in sorrow. As you have not died. (That's how you are here, alive, near this horse.)

You might not know this, but sometimes squirrels fall out of trees and they cry. They crawl to shelter and cry. Such a small brain, and yet, sorrow.

Are you shaken by this? Isn't the world a more horrible place now that you understand sorrow in one more way?

Like it's all the possible routes on a map and you have to learn them. You trace the line you've been on. You trace another nearby and think, *Whose death is this? Not my child's. Please. No. That bird's. Please. It looks like the outline of a wing.*

A child's hand, fingers together, is wing-like.

What's the scale of this map anyway? How many inches is how many miles of your life and your squandered happiness?

Jesus Christ, the map is a simile. The horse is real and drinking the water like it's the best water the world has to offer.

4.

It's getting late. The sun is in the trees with an edge as sharp as the line of the horse's back. Like it isn't sending out flares in solar storms all the time. Like it couldn't eat you up. And everything.

And, okay, maybe you pictured the bird wrong. It's easy to picture a wing out of place, some dirt where it shouldn't be. But you should know the bird's stomach was torn.

Listen, you won't get to see the sunset if you lie down here and try to sleep—see if you can forget all this.

The night would wake you up cold as shit, with everything a whole lot worse, if only because you wouldn't be able to make out your hands.

Also, an owl knows about the mouse.

Have you thought about what you will do if more animals are dead when you wake up? Can the horse be trusted to take care of herself?

You don't have to think about it. You didn't really want to go to sleep. The sun is gorgeous and you want to look at it until your eyes hurt. That's a fine way to spend this time.

5.

You think about how none of the animals come close to you. You think about how lonely it would be to stay out here, in terms of being touched.

You try to think about love, but you think about the last time you saw a vibrator, a condom, other objects.

You could use a shovel right now. Bury the bird. Wake up with a blister that needs tending.

Should you dig a hole with your bare hands? How deep does it even need to be? Afterwards, you could wash your hands in the stream.

Come to think of it, you're getting your bearings here.

Dig the hole, bury the bird, wash your hands, set up the tarp, go to sleep.

You're tired of looking at her.

6.

It won't be long before the bird is covered in maggots. And that's the image that will stick with you. You'll forget if she was a white bird or a black bird or a blue bird. That would be a shame.

And it might be too late. With her under the earth, you're dreaming about her covered in maggots.

But, unbeknownst to you, her little bird spirit is over your head.

Alive, she could barely get her tongue out of her mouth. Now, it's this silver ribbon that she's bringing up your arm.

She's confused at being underground. She's as much a fool as the mouse about how to give a body back.

The mouse—she has snuck beneath your belly for shelter and warmth.

7.

If only the night held one dream instead of many.

In the next dream you dig up the bird.

In the next dream you dig in the same place and find a gun. You've shot someone. You weren't supposed to return to this place where you hid the gun.

You're an idiot in your dream.

In the next dream the horse returns. The horse startles you awake. But you are still asleep. Dreams are some wicked things.

In the next dream you are in a desert. That's different.

You forget what grass is. What it smells like. What the shadows of trees look like across your legs.

You laugh your head off at the sight of a cactus.

In the next dream you can see the spirit of the bird that will haunt you for weeks. Her tongue makes you think all of her words will come out garbled.

Then you remember all she does is sing.

DAY 2

8.

Morning. Finally. You shake out your arms and legs. You want a way to make your chest feel limber. You think about the word *heartache*.

You try to remember if any of your dreams were about receiving a new heart.

True story: A group of mice, with healthy hearts, but getting transplants, were given hearts that were not a match, that would be rejected.

After the scientists thanked the doctors for their meticulous work, they played music for the mice.

They wanted to see which bodies, listening to what music, would reject their new hearts fastest. Slowest.

With no music, the mice died in a week. With shit music, almost two. With classical, three. With opera, four.

You think your body is rejecting your heart, new or not.

You think about how you don't know any opera.

You think about what it's like to have one week left to live and you start humming the first tune that pops into your head.

9.

The mouse has her morning routine. Scavenge. Scurry. Groom. Burrow. Then sleep for the day.

But she's thrilled at the sight of you.

She loves the structure of your arms. She's nothing but a muffled curve, but you're a series of points. Any time she looks at you, she sees how to make you out of stars.

Constellation of the Burier of Birds. Constellation of the Dreamer.

She might not burrow at all today.

At first she thought you'd be dangerous. She's heard stories of mice being fed to snakes, of mice dying in basements.

And she knows you might kill her yet.

10.

You decide to find the horse. Maybe there's enough of a chill in the morning air that her breath will puff out in clouds.

You don't bother to check your own breath.

A horse's body temperature is higher. 100 degrees, 101 even. That could make the difference.

You remember how a child once put his hand around the front of your neck and it made you feel nervous—nervous about your breath—despite yourself.

Despite your knowledge of your own strength.

You'd pictured yourself throwing the child, and you still feel bad about picturing that.

Like that makes you a terrible person.

There the horse is. She was looking for you too.

Her breath isn't in clouds.

You try to touch her by reaching a flat hand towards her nose. She doesn't resist you, and you get to feel her fur and the bone beneath it. But she nips at you.

You give her little pinches on her cheek and say, *No. No.*

11.

You missed it yesterday but now you can tell the horse is pregnant. You can see the foal moving inside her.

How did you miss it? Was the dead bird so distracting?

In this very moment, the bird spirit is wrapping her silver tongue around the horse's middle. If only she could speak, she would tell you the horse has been pregnant for eleven months.

She will foal this week.

There, see the droplets of milk on the inside of her leg. Her udder is full and ready. You think it's best not to touch the horse again.

She must know how to give birth in the grass.

You can't help but think about all the bones that are in her. And though they are covered in muscles and skin and fur, you hear a rattling sound that fills the woods.

12.

The bird spirit understands that her new form is more beautiful. Even if it is less seen.

And she flies so easily. Minutes ago she flew right under a bird of prey.

Hours ago she was above the clouds. The air was thin. The stars and moon were close.

Her body has been singing to her from under the earth.

The song is sad, and when she sings, a whistling noise leaves her torn stomach.

The mismatched notes of her grieving body are the saddest of all.

13.

You have to eat. The horse will be fine. Your stomach makes a noise, and the mouse appears.

You follow her to a tree where she climbs the roots.

Tied to a branch above you is a bear bag filled with food. You bring it down, decide how to ration it, and eat. There are a few pots and pans in the bag too.

That's not what's important. What's important is that the food was left. What's important is that there might be a bear in the woods.

You think of how a bear will eat every berry a hillside has to offer after waking from his long sleep. You think of how he fishes with his paws.

You think of how big you can make yourself appear.

You think of the pregnant horse until you are lost in thought.

The mouse climbs onto your shirt to eat the crumbs.

14.

You wash your hands in the stream. You're alone. There's not one animal that you can see.

You push the thought out of your head—fish in the water, worms in the dirt, ticks in the grass. Screw them.

The stream is noisier than you remember from last night. Noisier than you remember any stream you played in as a child.

Is that a function of childhood? The ever internal?

You remember lifting a rock, finding a crawfish, putting a small net behind him, and scaring him so he'd capture himself.

Your chest hurts in a way that reminds you of getting a headache in your ears. It's not a tightness. It's just misplaced.

You take your pulse in your neck.

The stream sounds like a heart without valves.

Something is caught on a branch, hanging over the water, way downstream.

15.

A kite. You take off your pants, socks, and shoes, and you wade into the stream.

After you pull the kite from the branches, you take it to a patch of sun. You lie in the grass where the drops of water on your legs twinkle like stars. Like your legs are twin galaxies.

Maybe an hour goes by. Maybe you drift off.

When you wake, you dress, unravel the kite's string, and go to a clearing. The mouse and the horse are with you now. They love the bright colors of the kite.

It takes quickly to the wind. The horse whinnies and you jump and the kite falls.

You forgot horses made noise. Regardless, you thought this one wasn't going to make any. You thought you knew her.

Everyone is a bit surprised is all.

You start again. The kite goes up and it's easy to hold on. The pull on the string is light and constant.

The kite's tail moves more. It twists one way. Then another.

16.

You let the kite pull you to the eastern edge of the clearing. And then you set out to run to the western edge with the kite in your hand.

That means the wind is blowing west to east. As if the wind fights the movement of the sun.

The clearing isn't large, but at the end of your run, you're panting. You bring a hand to your chest. You sit down.

The horse comes over to check on you. You laugh. You throw your arms back to brace yourself so you can throw your head back.

You stop laughing, but you don't bring your head up. The trees are behind you, and you see the sky clearly and you see it through branches.

Who's to say how far away the branches are? Who's to say how far away the sky is? Who spends their time measuring distances?

Is that an act of touching?

17.

The horse doesn't look at the sky. She's got you in her binocular vision and nearly every other damn thing in her monocular vision.

Looking at the sky is dizzying. You're steady. Around you is what she always sees. Grass, trees, where the two meet.

She understands every footfall in terms of its relationship to everything else, except the grass directly behind her. And even that she has a sense of, for having been there.

She's been thinking a lot about the phrase *beast of burden.*

She knows it doesn't refer to pregnancy, but as she's never pulled a cart or a plow, this is the first time it applies.

Her foal, if healthy, weighs 100 pounds inside of her. He or she will stand within an hour of being born. He or she will have the largest eyes of any land mammal.

And he or she—foal, baby, dearest—will grow to dread even the starry nights, how they're caught only in glimpses.

18.

Back to the bear bag to eat. Your need for food is usually nothing to you. Here it's annoying.

You could be running again, turning your body to breath.

You wonder if you should bathe in the stream. You wonder what bathing is without soap. You wonder what being dirty is when you're not getting into a bed at night.

The food is less annoying now that it's in pieces in your mouth. You feel the mush of crackers down between your teeth and cheek.

All of it feels good. Like there's a purpose to keeping yourself alive.

As you are hoisting the bag back to its place in the tree, the rope slips. How could you know it was the bird spirit licking your hands?

This is as much as she's figured out so far, of the abilities of her new form. And she's not trying to warn you about dying. She's not trying to thank you. She's not trying to tell you anything.

She's trying to name you.

19.

At the base of the tree where you keep the bear bag are twinflowers.

They're small, mostly white except for all the pink and purple mixed in. Their blooms hang upside down in little pairs.

You think about being tied to something. You think about smelling nice. You think about touching the moss on the tree. Then you do.

There are true twins and lovers and a mother with her firstborn baby. So many ways to imagine the twinflower as a symbol.

You try not to think about it like that, resembling humans, how their hearts ache towards another.

Your hand is still on the moss. You put your forehead to it and close your eyes.

This would be a nice place to sleep, if it didn't stink of food.

20.

You know of a good spot to watch the sunset. It's only a ten-minute walk back to the tarp.

So you get yourself there. You can see pretty far to the west. The sun is going to go down over a mountain. Another mountain.

It's not the same as watching it set over a lake—the reflection rippling up like everything's laughing—but it should be beautiful.

You can also see you have a good twenty minutes before the sky really starts to do its thing. You decide to carve your initials into a tree.

You've been carrying around a spoon you found in the bear bag, and you find a nice flat rock.

First you scoop the bark off in chunks. Then you clear the area completely by scraping the spoon over it again and again. It's not a bad sound, how some scraping is.

Now you put the end of the spoon against the trunk, knock the other end with the rock, and you make a small mark.

You make a lot of small marks. You turn around and the sky is bright pink.

You're glad the sun is going to spend time every day shining on you. This version of you that will outlast your body.

If you knew how to better represent yourself than with two crap-carved letters, well Jesus, you would do that.

21.

You've seen sunsets. This one was like those. Pink, purple, yellow, orange. Then all of a sudden the sky is dark blue. Then all of a sudden there are stars.

You know they're far. You think of that distance in terms of time. You can't help yourself.

You know in one way you will live a number of years. In another way you live the distance the Earth traveled during that time.

And if you are emitting any light, as you often hope you are, then that light travels out another distance, another length of time.

You are living for centuries. You are living forever.

As you turn to leave, you say, *Goodnight*. You open your mouth. You close your mouth. You're constantly eating light.

22.

As you head back to the tarp, you see the bear. You don't know if she sees you.

If she does, she doesn't care. She's walking to where she will sleep for the night.

You hide behind a tree. You can hear her walking. Why hadn't you heard her before?

You try to calm down. You try to focus. You hold your breath.

You hear other sounds you've been ignoring. Coyotes you think. But far away.

What other animals are out there? Bobcats? Let them sleep. You're so tired.

Shit, where's the bear? Does this mean you can go back or does this mean you have to stay put?

You don't know how to make a decision. You're shaking.

The bird spirit has learned how to make a glimmer in the dark. She's trying to guide you home.

If you would just look up. If you would just open your eyes.

The bird spirit wonders what's wrong with you. You've been in this much trouble the whole time.

23.

Back under the tarp, you fall asleep. You worry you will dream of being mauled by a bear, but don't worry.

In the first dream you're sleeping next to someone. Warm. Soft. Breathing well.

Then that person wakes up and yells, *Oh no*, like something's been forgotten. Like the night is full of reminders.

Like the night will never let you forget anything.

In the next dream you're sleeping next to someone you can't wake.

In the next dream you're sleeping next to someone whose leg is across yours and it arouses you.

In the next dream you're sleeping next to someone and you're about to speak, maybe whisper a name, when the mouse comes to you, chattering in your ear.

But it's not the mouse. It's rain, hitting the tarp.

DAY 3

24.

You were ready for this. The tarp is set up between two trees, angled towards the ground, as a lean-to.

You have two choices. Try to stay dry all day under the tarp. Or leave your clothes to be dry and spend your day naked in the woods.

Your hunger makes the decision for you. You get undressed.

You wrap your underwear in your shirt, your shirt in your sweater, your sweater in your pants, which should be a little tougher if the wind blows any rain in.

Outside the tarp, the mouse is playing in a puddle. But she stops when she sees you.

She thinks your body looks like a collection of nests. She better understands your clothes now as a way of keeping your body for yourself.

You don't know how to understand your modesty.

25.

When clouds cover the sky, then is it one cloud? Cloudscape. It's such a dark gray. Like slate and tar. But it only means that it's full of water.

Do all clear things turn dark when piled on top of each other? If you covered yourself in enough rain, would you get dark enough to hide in a fire's smoke?

You just described drowning. The smoky bodies at the bottoms of the lakes and seas. Don't you understand light, light-eater?

At least the bear won't roam around today. She's in a cave with her snout under her paw.

And the bird spirit is thrilled that it's so dark because she can practice her new skill. Soon she'll be able to make her outline appear, and you won't question if you see her.

You run your left hand down your right arm. The rain sloughs off.

26.

Your body is so wet that finding dry spots under trees feels like you've wandered out of your natural habitat and might die.

You have a new body that's perfect for the rain.

You're an alien. You develop a new walk that's mostly shuffling. You start saying the beeps of your new language.

You think, *I'm home*, for the first time in a long time. You translate, *I'm home*, into beeps and scream it out into the rain.

You have thirty-seven different words for rain. This rain can be described in one word but it translates loosely to:

good smelling hard falling rain that makes you feel like shiny beetles are hiding everywhere and you are keeping two of the shiniest ones in your heart

27.

You find the horse tucked away under a tree thick with branches.
Your alien self is less afraid of her half-ton body.

You shuffle over to her and you beep and you laugh and shake water
out of your hair.

Her tail whips up from the ground for an instant. She's got one eye
on you but you know that means the other eye is seeing the movements
in her belly.

You wonder how her brain presents herself with all she sees—
panoramic or split screen or alternating or . . . Is it maddening?

Does split vision further split the brain? Does it develop two
personalities? One the quiet horse and one the horse who whinnies
at the kite?

You can never know her. She's impossible to know.

For her, the longer you stand there, the longer you're paired with
the image of her foal in the womb. And she becomes uncomfortable
with this.

28.

You lie down in the rain. You've been rushing through this day as an alien. Time to return to being a human, to having a tongue and lips that make hundreds of sounds.

You keep your eyes closed against the rain. You pick an area of your body—the palm of your right hand—and you try to count the rain drops that land there.

You hated reading that book on palm reading. The lifeline on your left hand curves around to your wrist like everyone else's. But the lifeline on your right hand stops halfway down.

What does that even mean? Die at 25? At 50? Become ill? Be tested? Get stuck in the woods? Does it mean stop trying? Don't have a child? Because isn't your first promise not to die?

What was that? 600. 610 rain drops on your right palm. 620. 621, 22, 23. You're counting too fast to say anything out loud.

29.

It's happened. You're tired of the rain. You're tired of being wet and naked. You're tired of the pat-down dirt and glistening trees.

The ground is covered in puddles. They take the shapes of animals the same way clouds do.

You snort at the hippopotamus puddle. You spot a dragon and kick the water out like it's breathing fire. What's to stop you from being happy here?

You shake a branch and watch the water fall from it.

Then you see the bird spirit. She's come back to haunt you. Her disgustingly long tongue. All in silver. She's flying in circles around you.

You've heard some people stay as ghosts because they don't know what's happened to them.

You yell, *You're dead, bird! You died!*

It comes out sounding cruel.

30.

You can't outrun a ghost. You're not even sure if she'd chase you, or just reappear back where you sleep.

You're not sure what you can offer a ghost either. No fruit. No shelter. No soft touch on her wing.

What does she want? You did right by her, burying her. She won't be picked over for weeks until her little bones are bare and falling away from each other.

But she's scaring you. Her inability to receive anything scares you. You're watching the rain pass through her.

You go over it again. You can't run. You can't hold her. Fight her. Gift her. You start shaking. Like last night. But as far as you know, the bird can't harm you.

You start jumping up and down. You start shaking harder than you're shaking. You shake your hips. You start dancing.

You bet the bird has never seen dancing. You can teach her. Maybe it will fill her with joy and she'll go.

Maybe it will fill her with joy and that tiny silver frame can explode all over these woods and leave you the hell alone.

31.

The bird spirit can tell you're doing this for her. She does a quick turn in the air.

She turns with her wings out. She turns twice in a row. She puts one wing out and then the other and so on.

She likes this. She likes you. She has no idea what she wants.

To be felt. To be seen. Easy enough. But now what? She could go anywhere.

She could travel to Mars, but she's just a bird. She doesn't know how stunning her ghost would be on the Red Planet.

She feels like she needs to be taken care of. She thinks you could be the one to do that for her.

God knows why. Look at you.

You're holding your nose, waving your arm, bending your knees, and pretending you're sinking to the bottom of the ocean.

32.

Your fear has receded. So what a ghost? So what a bear? So what inimitable loneliness at the sight of twinflowers? So what?

You stop dancing and set out for the tarp. Your stomach is full and before you sleep, you'll spend a few hours dressed and hidden.

The ghost might be there, sure. It'll be less dark. Less lonely. Even if she can't be touched. Even if her tongue sickens you.

Maybe you'll get used to it. Maybe she needs you. Maybe, as her needs are met, her tongue will shrink. You'll watch it rise and fall in her beak. A light she's keeping safe.

Maybe she could go into your chest and figure out what's wrong with your heart.

How do you ask her to do something like that? How do you describe a healthy heart to a bird?

A sleeping red dove.

33.

If you tell a bird that a heart is like a bird without wings, she will tell you it is broken because it doesn't have wings.

Back under the tarp you dry off the best you can and get back in your clothes. You feel warm and for a second you mistake that for all the happiness in the world.

The mouse breaks through the dirt near your feet. Maybe she can teach you to be pleased with the small space under the tarp.

You sit down and hold your hand out to her. She crawls up, up to your elbow and back down into your hand. She looks at you.

How is it every animal understands an invitation?

You start to tell her about your day. You warn her the bird is coming, in case something like that would startle her. When you're done talking, you lower your hand.

Before she scurries off, she nips you hard beneath your thumb. She wants to remind you she is a wild thing.

34.

The blood comes up and hesitates in a dome on your skin. You know that's surface tension at work. You imagine a microscopic water bug moving across your blood droplet.

You roll up your sleeve and stick your hand outside of the tarp and let the rain clean you. You bring your arm back in and apply pressure.

It's not much of a bite. Though it's your first bite in a very long time.

You were once told a girl bit your cheek in preschool. If that had scarred, would it have shrunk on your growing face? Or would it have expanded, always able to fit around your cheek?

Did you know about blood at that age? You know too much now. Sometimes when you're falling asleep you trace its path:

Into the top right of your heart. Out of the bottom right and into the lungs. Back to the top left. Out of the bottom left and to the rest of the body.

You usually run your fingers up your neck when you think about that last part.

35.

You wonder if this is how any human body would live in the woods. You know that some mice build escape tunnels and some do not and that's located in their genes.

And that's all you're asking. Are you the type to not build the tunnel, and is there someone else who would?

A picture of one mouse's escape tunnel showed how the mouse paused right before breaking through the ground. How clever is that?

You imagine a snake slithering into the mouse's nest. And there's no second snake, smart and waiting, at the other end, because no one but the mouse knows where the other end is.

You're lying to yourself. You don't care if someone else would build the tunnel. You care if it's your fault that you haven't. Or if it's been in your blood for generations.

You tap on a bit of earth and hear the same thick sound as ever.

36.

Then you realize snakes aren't teaming up on mice.

So why not two complete tunnels? A flat-out getaway. You consider a mouse preparing for this scenario—these two predators attacking at once.

God, you hadn't considered that for yourself.

What if the bear is to one side of you and a bobcat leaps at you from another? Why not?

Your current escape plan is to run like hell to the bear bag where you can throw food and arm yourself with a frying pan.

That's the most you want to think about it, in case thinking about it makes it happen.

Earlier you thought about the bird and then her ghost appeared.

You thought about worms and then they were everywhere.

You thought about a coyote and then you heard one.

37.

If you have so much power, then you should think about what you do want. List them. Think them twice.

The rain to stop. The sun to come out. A rainbow even.

Butterflies that come and land on your hands.

The mouse to apologize and take back her stupid red bite.

The horse to come to you wanting to be held.

A person to touch. A baby too. A home.

This is bad. You can't think about this. This makes you cry. You kept these clothes dry all day and now you're ruining your sleeves on your face.

You're sobbing. You're doing that strange choking between sobs. This could be an anxiety attack.

It's not necessarily despair.

38.

You know you will feel better in the morning. And you will fall asleep more easily after all this crying.

You try to relax. You empty your pockets and line up your belongings in front of you in the dim light.

A spoon. A bent playing card (not a face card—a number). A flat rounded stone you've been carrying around from the stream.

Then you pretend to lay out the things you should have with you.

A pocket knife. A flashlight. A comb. A compass. A whistle. A map. A pen. A wrist watch. Tissues. Matches.

You outline them with the spoon. Except for the compass's circle, they're a bunch of rectangles in the dirt.

And you lie down to sleep among your riches.

39.

Tonight, in every dream, you are an animal.

First you are a ram. You want to run into everything with your new horns. You start with another ram. You make an enemy to know your strength, and you would make more.

Next you are an elk. You like looking down at your hooves from this height. You get dizzy and laugh. You like the tracks you make through the woods.

Next you are the pregnant horse. Why her? The foal kicks you with her unborn legs. You feel like you have to pee. This is an anticlimactic dream.

Next you are a fish. That's better. You let the new parts of your neck comb through the water for oxygen. You open and close your mouth in the same shape over and over.

You can't keep track anymore. The scenes are changing too quickly. You are a shapeless phenom.

40.

The last dream is overly specific.

You are a wolf pup taken in by a horse who has recently miscarried. She nurses you. She fears you will never love her as much as she loves you.

You have the same fear. You have a wolf's howl.

You shouldn't understand abandonment but you do.

Her coat of fur is black and yours is gray. You feel as if she is the night sky and you are a cloud and together you're obscuring something like the moon. And that's good.

It feels very good to know what kind of light you can hold between the two of you.

The horse lets you lie beside her and you forget everything you're supposed to forget.

It feels like the last dream you'll ever have.

DAY 4

41.

When you wake, the rain has stopped. Everything is wet and still smells of rain, but the sun is so bright. What a relief. What a wonder.

You hurry to the stream. The flooding has stranded some fish in puddles and you catch one. You strike it with a rock.

You probably shouldn't eat it raw but it tastes good. Better than the old food from the bear bag. Not that you aren't thankful.

You eat some berries too. You drink some water. You sit at a giant rock and pretend you are at a restaurant.

You snap your fingers at a waiter. You motion for the check.
You tip well.

Next you want to see the horse. See if the sun is greeting her as well as it seems to have met you this morning. As it seems to beckon you from one shining piece of this world to the next.

42.

The horse is under the tree where she was yesterday. She's pacing and switching her tail, and you watch her from a distance.

As a child you misheard switching as swishing. But looking at her now, switching is a better match. Switching is a deliberate action.

Swishing is being caught up in winds that make dried leaves dance. And we're so much heavier than leaves.

Watching her like this, you realize the horse is more beautiful than you'd like her to be. You'd like her to be plain, approachable.

You'd like to think that you could take a picture of her and say, *Yes, to be close to her was seeing her just as you see her here.*

Finally you go to her. She lowers her head in your direction and paws at the ground. You would be scared, but you know immediately what's happening.

Today she will give birth to her foal.

43.

She could be like this for hours before anything happens. Before she might need your help. So you leave her.

One of your earliest memories is asking your mother to pick you up and her explaining that she can't over her pregnant belly. You remember her belly. You remember your mother. You were two.

You don't know this but the horse is four. She got pregnant when she was three.

She could live another fifteen years out here. She could see another five thousand sunrises, another five thousand sunsets. Be aware of the turning of the Earth another ten thousand times.

It sounds like a lot but you've already lived that long and it was nothing. It was rising from bed.

44.

You don't know what to do with yourself. You want soap. You want clean hands to touch the foal later.

Next to the stream, you set up two flat rocks. One larger than the other.

With your spoon, you dig up a dozen small plants and their roots. Some roots are woody, some waxy, some don't look big enough to sustain the blossoms above.

You smash them between the rocks and throw water on them and take them in your hands to see if anything lathers.

Okay, maybe you don't know much about soap. Maybe you wasted an hour. Maybe your hands are dirtier than when you started.

Maybe you'll discover that one of these roots bursts into stars. One into a hundred white worms.

45.

The bird spirit appears and you tell her about the coming foal. She knows, but she likes your excitement.

You tell her how your heart is feeling better. How you've been thinking about the foal for hours, and usually thinking that much about a child would ruin you, but here you are, covered in dirt and full of purpose.

She doesn't understand your heart. How it is your partner in the functioning of your living body, and yet, you seem to become uncoupled in moments of urgency. It betrays you. It's begun to silver, beating inside of you.

She touches your chest with her tongue and you jump.

When she touches you there again, you're able to stay still.

46.

Should you be preparing for the worst? Dig a grave the size of the foal?
Dig a grave the size of the horse?

Would their ghosts follow you too? Could you stand it?

You shake your head. You kneel at the stream and splash water on your
face. Your pants get wet in the mud where your knees fall.

The dark spots call attention to the discreteness of your body.
Must everything?

You think of the horse. Even knowing that she is two horses right now,
she looks more whole than you do.

You remember staying up late with a pregnant rabbit one night, when
it was clear she was about to give birth. (This was part of your old life.)

All at once, she began tearing the fur from her chest and belly. She was
noisy and you were scared for her.

She birthed many rabbits that night into that soft nest of herself, and
all survived.

47.

Yes, the bunnies did well, but you also remember the ducklings.

One had trouble getting out of her shell, and as you helped off that last stuck piece, she began to bleed.

And then you had that wet, bleeding duckling in the palm of your hand. You held her under the heat lamp for hours.

And then she was fine. Clearly the runt, but fine.

But later you heard that the whole group was moved to a farm, and she died. Or was killed.

You imagined how she stood out in the group. And though every duck seems easy to kill, more so the weaker one.

You could not bring yourself to think that was the life appropriate to her. The length of her life matching the shortcomings of her body.

But the horse is not a duck. The foal will never be held. The body will reek of strength.

48.

Everything will go well, you tell yourself. Today is an amazing day to be born! The spring is amazing! The wind and grass and trees! The animals twittering!

Today the foal will continue this misplaced lineage—not wild horse but descendant of the feral Spanish horses brought here hundreds of years ago.

And then escaped? Owners killed? Owners tricked and stolen from in the night?

Owners feeling bad in the face of so much land? Slapping hindquarters and yelling, *Gid-yap!* Except in Spanish. Not the slurring cowboy you imagine.

Did someone wake and say, *Dónde están los caballos?* Or, *Dónde está mi caballo?*

You have caught yourself in the past hours referring to the horse as your own. *My horse this . . . My horse that . . .*

But she is not yours, and you would do well to remember that.

49.

If the horse were in Spain, she would be in a stable. Men and women and children would situate themselves on her back, one leg against one side, one leg against the other.

They would measure her and describe her size in metrics. They would watch for her breath in her flank, so far back in the body. They would be there for her when she foals.

Maybe she would have been taken to run on beaches of the Atlantic. An ocean you have run along too.

You think you will tell the foal every story you know of her rich Spanish history. Then you change your mind.

You can't imagine one more animal looking at these woods, full of the glory of the sun, and thinking they do not belong.

50.

You return to the horse. She's still pacing. She's kicking at her abdomen. She's positioning the foal.

There's a wet spot in the dirt. It's all about to start. It has started. So many starting points.

She doesn't mind that you're here. It feels like she doesn't notice you, but of course she does. She can smell you. She can smell everything. Even the ghost.

The ghost smells like a wind that came in off the ocean. And she guesses that ghosts are salty.

At first she thinks of the ghost as uninhabitable, a hostile environment. No wonder the empty silver outline. No wonder the lack of stomach, brain, the hot heart.

Then she remembers the creatures in the sea. The waves. The waves. And she relaxes. She lies down. The foal begins to emerge.

51.

The foal comes out head first in a giant sac. Or the foal is giant but the sac makes her appear more giant. It looks as if the horse is dividing herself in half.

The foal raises her head and the sac breaks and fluid is everywhere.

The horse looks like she might stand again. You shoot her a look that you think says, *I'll kill you if you break that baby in half.*

The horse sees it as, *I might pass out if you stand up with half of a foal hanging out of you.*

She extends her back legs. Then the foal's hips are out. Then her back legs. There's so much fluid.

The foal is perfect.

And the timing begins. The foal must stand in the hour. The placenta must be out in three. You look at where the sun is—everything should be resolved by dark.

52.

Already the foal stands. As she does, the umbilical cord breaks.

You walk over, take the cord, and tie it to a low branch. The pull of it is supposed to help the placenta come out whole.

The horse is covered in sweat. She loves the sight of her foal. She whinnies in her direction.

She tries to ignore you. How you slip by her. How you look at the foal as if you love her. How the cord left smears of blood across your palms and fingers. Her blood or the foal's—she's not sure.

She doesn't know if their blood is different at all. You know. You know they are two distinct bodies.

But that's a feeling the horse is having just now for the very first time.

53.

Soon the foal is trotting. She trots around the trunk of the tree. You follow. You cheer her on. You're smiling so big your face should break off.

You remember galloping as a child. You remember your father slapping his thigh between a smooth kind of clap over his leg, and there was the rhythm of a horse in the living room or in the kitchen.

He told you stories of horses. He told you how he made small braids in the manes of horses. Memories you'd forgotten.

The horse starts extending her legs again. She's distressed and makes noises to match.

The feelings you have for the foal feel like feelings for the horse. You go right up to her and pat her on her neck. You tell her that she will be okay. And, staying beside her, you put a quick braid in her hair, selfish as that is.

And then the placenta is out. Not thick. No signs of hemorrhage. Nothing missing. With an hour of sunlight left, the horse gets up to meet her foal.

The placenta lies on the ground. With the cord tied to a branch, you want it to look like an upside-down flower, like a magnified microscopic organism with its flagellum stuck in a tree. Like something beautiful or magical, at least surprising. Because it looks like trauma.

You have to look at the nursing foal to have any real sense of well-being.

54.

The mouse is here. The bird spirit too. Everyone is overjoyed at the foal's arrival.

But the horse, newly acquainted with the distance between herself and the foal, is not happy about any of you.

She stamps her hooves at the mouse until she runs off. She rears up at the ghost. She's so much bigger than everyone, so much more muscular. You have underestimated her again.

The bird spirit backs away out of respect, because she sees grief in the horse, because the fear of loss is enough.

The horse seems to calm down, circling her foal. But she is not calm. She's getting into the right spot.

She kicks you in the chest.

You fall and cough blood. You watch as she pushes the foal out from under the tree to a new part of the woods.

55.

As soon as the horses are gone, the mouse returns. She weeps over you.

The bird spirit disappears into your body. You didn't need to ask.

You roll onto your stomach and crawl out from under the tree. You'd hate to die where a birth took place, to contaminate one with the other. More honestly, you'd hate to die near the placenta, the size of a baby itself.

You get to grass and roll again. You look at the clouds. You look at the blue around them. *Better*, you think.

You think, *This is what a cracked sternum feels like.* A broken rib, a punctured lung, blood pooling inside you like you're finally the vessel the Church describes.

The mouse undoes the laces of your boots and you kick them off.

The bird spirit returns to where you can see her, but instead of giving you any news, any hope, she sings.

56.

The horse surprised herself. But she also thinks, *Good riddance.* She understands riddance.

Then the questions begin. Will she be able to avoid that part of the woods? Will she be stuck with your decaying body for weeks? You buried the bird, but who will bury you?

Surely she can avoid you, your darkening flesh. But what of the foal? Teach him already that there are places to go and places not to? Teach him, *forbidden.* Teach him already, *death.*

What if she needs you? What if you would help keep the bear from the foal? What if you would sacrifice your life when she would sacrifice her own, and she could go on living?

But how sick she would feel, if the foal grew to love you. If she let you ride her. If she galloped when you kicked. If she stopped at a sound from your human throat.

57.

It's hard to know how long it will take to die.

The sunset is almost boring when you can't see the horizon. When you're stuck looking at one chunk of blue that slowly blackens. Slowly lets out stars.

Only it's not boring, because when would you have watched it like this before? Had so much patience? Held your head so still?

Injury lends a certain steadiness. Like your whole life was spent uneasy in your body. And now it's sighing, *At last. At last.*

You want to comfort the mouse. You hold out your hand and she runs up your arm and curls into a ball on your chest.

She feels your heartbeat in every hair on her belly. For every one of your heartbeats she has six.

She wonders how much of your life she can swallow up. Does she not breathe more breaths? Does she not beat more beats?

Does she not express desire as best she knows how?

58.

More animals come because of your new smell and the smell of the nearby afterbirth.

They hesitate when they see that it's you. They investigate the placenta and return to the others with blood on their paws, with blood on their mouths.

Maybe they're hesitating because the bird spirit is making herself huge—she's around your whole body. You look at her silver head above your head. She whips her tongue at them.

You don't know if you're more scared of the coyotes who will work together tonight, or the bear who works alone.

The bear is taking her time to join the group of gathered animals. You want to feel her heavy steps across the earth.

The animals form a circle around you, and the coyotes walk around the edge of it. You are a spectacle.

59.

It's getting very dark. The bird spirit's head is as bright as the moon.

You spray blood from your mouth so you can watch the red mist catch the light of the ghost, and it does. You think you hear an animal gasp.

It's hard to keep yourself from dreaming. And contemplating what's real seems like a fool's errand.

You hear one coyote say, *Isn't it a shame?* And another blurts out, *That we didn't come here sooner!* And the rest laugh.

Even you are laughing. What jokesters! To be eaten days ago!

You see their white teeth flashing in the night by the light of the ghost.

The horse couldn't come back now even if she wanted to. So you imagine she wants to.

60.

You hear the calls of the bird and the scratching feet of the mouse. She's trying to get to your heart.

You hear the coyotes begin to howl. You hear the deep growl of the bear. You hear bobcats pawing at the ground.

Very far off, you hear the horse breathing. You hear the foal breathing. You hear their planetary hearts.

You feel their gravitational pull. How is anyone still standing? How is anyone still living their lives?

You hear the wind, the branches, the stream, the moon. You hear everything moving closer to the hearts of the horses.

You hear the world collapse. It sounds like singing a child to sleep. Which is to say, the song gets softer.

ART

by Nicky Arscott

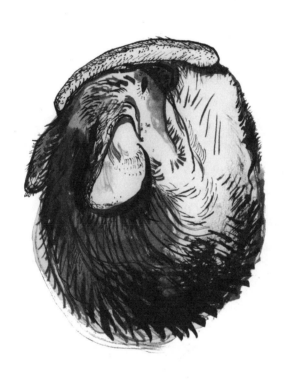

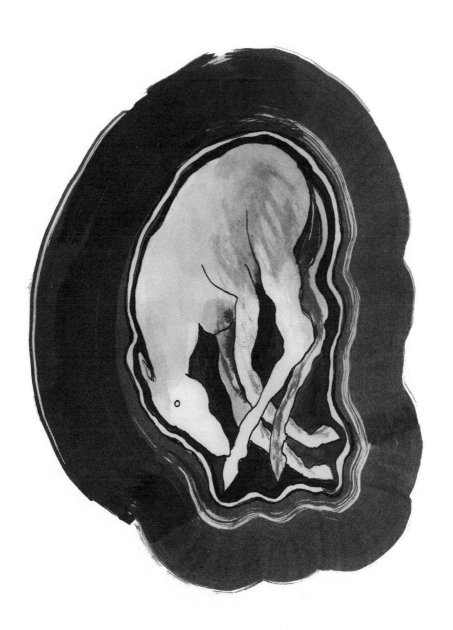

ACKNOWLEDGMENTS

Sincere thanks to the editors of the following journals, who published many of these poems, often in earlier versions, under the title, "In a Wood, with Clearings, It's Spring":

Ampersand Review: 14 and 15
Jellyfish Poetry: 11 and 12
The Los Angeles Review of Books: 20 through 49
The Mondegreen: 6 and 7

Thank you to my family, especially my mom and dad, who might think that this is the best poem I've ever written.

Thank you to Aaron, who changed how my mind works. I wrote this entire poem on my phone by his side when he was one year old.

Thank you to Nicky Arscott for her incredible artwork.

Thank you to my friends who have read and supported my work over the years—Catie Rosemurgy, Lynne Beckenstein, Linda Gallant, Rachel Mennies, Natalie Shapero, Eleanor Stanford, Kimberly Quiogue Andrews, Maximiliano Schell, Evan McGarvey, Shane McCrae, Sarah Yake, Todd Davis, Julia Kasdorf, Kathleen Ossip, Amorak Huey, Joe Ahearn, Noah Schoenholtz, and Gabrielle Calvocoressi. Thank you, too, to Anieszka Banks, who illustrated parts of this poem many years ago.

Enormous thank you to Suzanna Tamminen, Stephanie Prieto, and the rest of the team at Wesleyan University Press. And thank you to the National Endowment for the Arts.